i'm not

51 musings to arouse your curiosity,

done

stir your soul, remind you what is possible,

growing

and nourish your mind!

yet

MATTHEW KELLY

BLUE
sparrow

To learn more about the author, visit:
MatthewKelly.com

The-Best-Version-of-Yourself and 60 Second Wisdom
are registered trademarks.

ISBN: 978-1-63582-256-4 (hardcover)

Designed by Ashley Dias

10   9   8   7   6   5   4   3   2   1

FIRST EDITION

Printed in the United States of America

table
of
contents

introduction: keep growing

Are you growing?

Growing requires effort and intentionality. It doesn't just happen.

This is true in every area of our lives. I experienced it professionally last year. For years people had been encouraging me to get into YouTube. For years, I resisted. I'm not sure why. Perhaps just too many opportunities to do other things. Perhaps a bias toward a live audience after almost 30 years on the road.

But in the early months of last year, with the help of a small team, I started exploring the world of YouTube. We started by posting video content from my archives. Mostly live events and interviews. I wanted to get a sense of what content would resonate with viewers.

Almost immediately I was awestruck at the power of the tool we call YouTube. It was fascinating in new and different ways every day for months.

We learn from other people. Throughout history, people have gone to certain places to exchange ideas. Tribes gathered to hear from elders and sages. Religious groups gathered to hear from priests and rabbis. Ancient Greeks, from Aristotle to Alexander the Great, attended Plato's academy. Over time and in different places, people would gather in town squares, marketplaces, baths, coffeehouses, inns, and universities.

All of these were bound by the limitations of space and time. You could not go to the town square to discuss a topic with someone who was there one hundred years ago. You were also limited by geography. You could not go to the town square of a village a thousand miles away. And you certainly could not go to all the town squares.

Books and libraries were a marvelous advance in this sense. They allowed us to share the ideas of great thinkers from every place and time.

YouTube is now one of the primary venues where the modern exchange of ideas takes place.

On August 4th, 2021, we released my first video that was specifically made for YouTube, and we have released at least one new video every day since.

More than one thousand videos later, and 15 million views in more than one hundred countries, I continued to be amazed by how far and wide these messages are being experienced. The positive feedback of viewers is encouraging. The negative feedback of viewers helps me to hone the skill of reaching people where they are in their journey.

From the very beginning, we received thousands of comments and emails requesting transcripts of various videos, so we started posting them on my blog.

Those first months will always be a fond memory of something new, exciting, and fulfilling.

I love books, and so, the idea emerged to pull together this volume. Between these covers, you will find fifty-one of the transcripts from the early days of this adventure.

Book titles either come to me very quickly, early on in the process, or they allude me until the end. The title for this book had been alluding me throughout, until I was sitting in a meeting one day. A colleague was describing a conversation he had with a friend. He was sharing with his friend how frustrated he was with himself, because life wasn't unfolding the way he hoped it would. His friend said to him, "But you're not done growing yet, right?"

And there it was. I had my title. I'm not done growing yet. You're not done growing yet.

Some of these readings will no doubt be of more interest to you than others. But if you look closely, I hope you will discover that every single one of these short texts can help you grow. And to grow is a wonderful thing. It fills us with energy and enthusiasm, satisfaction and hope for the future.

The older I get the more I realize how essential encouragement is to each and every single one of us. When I sit down to write, I see it as one of my primary goals and responsibilities.

One of my favorite quotes is from the Talmud. It reads, "Every blade of grass has its own angel that bends over it and whispers, 'Grow?' 'Grow!'"

The secret to so many things seems simply to be: Keep growing! May today's self be an improvement on yesterday's self. There is something immensely satisfying about that.

MATTHEW KELLY

1.
do you want to live a meaningful life?

You cannot live a meaningful life by filling your life with meaningless things and activities.

The secret to living a meaningful life is to strip away everything that is meaningless. Strip away anything that is trivial or unnecessary and everything left will be meaningful.

If living a meaningful life depends on filling our lives with meaningful activity, ask yourself: Who are the people, things, and activities that help you weed out the meaningless from the meaningful?

Who helps you prioritize what matters most and gives you the courage to say no to what matters least?

We say we want to live more meaningful lives, but we keep saying yes to meaningless things. Start saying no to meaningless things and a more meaningful and fulfilling life will emerge. It has no choice.

There is no secret to living a meaningful life. Fill your life with meaningful relationships, experiences, work, and things... and your life will become more meaningful. It has no choice.

2.
busy is
not
your friend

Busy is not your friend. It makes you feel overwhelmed, tired, and inadequate. If busy were a person, would you spend all day with that person today, and then all day with that person again tomorrow? I don't think so.

Busy is not your friend. They say judge a tree by its fruits. Well, the fruits of busy are overwhelmed, weary, tired, burned out, worn-out, resentful, discouraged, anxious, and stressed. Which of these fruits do you want in your life?

When asked: "What one word would you use to describe how you feel on a daily basis?" millions of people say overwhelmed.

How often do you feel overwhelmed?

Do you feel like there aren't enough hours in the day to get everything done?

Are you overwhelmed with things that really matter or things that won't mean anything to anyone in a couple of weeks?

When we are overwhelmed with things we know don't really matter, we become resentful. So, it's not just that we are busy, but that we are busy with the wrong things.

We all know the feeling of exhaustion at the end of a day when you have worked hard on the right things. There is satisfaction in that tiredness.

But we also know the exhaustion that comes from doing lots of nothing important. This exhaustion is heavy and draining.

Busy leads to overwhelmed, overwhelmed leads to weary, weary leads to discouraged, and discouragement leads us to feel inadequate and resentful. Anyone or anything that makes you feel that way is too small for you.

Busy is not your friend. Keep that in mind next time you feel pressured to say yes to something you know you should say no to.

3.
who
would
hide you?

How do you measure your life? It's good to weigh our lives from time to time. It ensures we are not wasting our one short life. But there are so many ways to measure a life: success, family and relationships, career, money, status, stuff, education, popularity, integrity, happiness, adventure, health...

What measuring stick do you use to assess your life? Here's a perspective I had never considered: A Polish Holocaust survivor once told Warren Buffet, "Warren, I'm very slow to make friends, because when I look at people, the question I ask is: Would they hide me?"

There is no perfect way to measure our lives. But these two questions are worth considering:

If you were in trouble, being hunted unjustly, how many people do you know who would risk their lives to hide you? And the second question, how many people would you be willing to hide?

4.
how to predict your future?

Predicting your future is easy. Sure, there are some aspects of the future that are impossible to know, and everyone gets surprised by life sometimes, but for the most part, life is highly predictable. Would you like me to predict your future? I would rather teach you how to predict your own.

Tell me four things:

What do you spend more time thinking about than anything else?

Describe the character of the five people you spend most time with.

What books do you plan to read in the next 12 months?

What are your habits, the things you do every day?

Answer these, and you can predict your future,

because what we think about always increases in our life. Sooner or later, we all rise or fall to the level of our friendships. We become the books we read. And our habits shape our destiny.

If you don't like what you see when you look into the future, change these four things.

5.
what's your dream?

One of your most amazing abilities is your ability to dream. You can stand here, look into the future, imagine something bigger or better, and then chase it down and make it happen. That's an amazing ability.

So, here's my question for you today: What are your dreams?

This question takes most people off guard because, at some point, most of us stopped dreaming. We get into survival mode, get absorbed with the daily realities of life, put other people's dreams ahead of our own, and wake up one day and wonder what happened.

Today is that day. Time to wake up. Your dreams are your dreams for a reason. Time to dream again. Grab a piece of paper and make a list of ten things you would love to do. Don't judge your dreams, just write them down. Then pick one—big or small—and get after it.

The future can be better than the past, and you can do something today to bring that about. So, whatever your dream is, get after it!

6.
24 regrets of people dying

What do people regret when they are dying? I asked hospice nurses. Here are the top 24 regrets people have when they are dying:

I wish I'd had the courage to just be myself.

I wish I had spent more time with the people I love.

I wish I had made spirituality more of a priority.

I wish I hadn't spent so much time working.

I wish I had discovered my purpose earlier.

I wish I had learned to express my feelings more.

I wish I hadn't spent so much time worrying about things that never happened.

I wish I had taken more risks.

I wish I had cared less about what other people thought.

I wish I had realized earlier that happiness is a choice.

I wish I had loved more.

I wish I had taken better care of myself.

I wish I had been a better spouse.

I wish I had paid less attention to other people's expectations.

I wish I had quit my job and found something I really enjoyed doing.

I wish I had stayed in touch with old friends.

I wish I had spoken my mind more.

I wish I hadn't spent so much time chasing the wrong things.

I wish I'd had more children.

I wish I had touched more lives.

I wish I had thought about life's big question earlier.

I wish I had traveled more.

I wish I had lived more in the moment.

I wish I had pursued more of my dreams.

These are the regrets of people who were out of time. Some people think it's morbid to think about death. I disagree. It's healthy to think about death. It puts things in perspective and reminds us what really matters. The inevitability of death should inspire us to get busy living.

7.
your
LOVE
contract

Do you ever feel like you can't figure yourself out? There is one question that will provide more insight into who you are, why you do the things you do, and how you participate in relationships than all the other questions put together.

This is the question: What did you have to do to receive love as a child?

Most people aren't aware of it, but we all sign a love contract when we are young. For better or for worse, the people who raise us teach us about the giving and receiving of love. And most of us are still living according to that contract today.

Did you have to do as you were told? Did you have to accomplish things? Were you taught that love involves a quid pro quo exchange, that it was transactional? Did you have to hide your true feelings and emotions? Did you have to keep your opinions to yourself? Or perhaps you were you loved simply for who you are?

Go deep into this question and you will discover yourself in ways that will astound you. It will reveal extraordinary insights into your relationships, past and present.

What did you have to do to receive love as a child? Whatever it was, you have probably kept doing it your whole life. And depending on how healthy or dysfunctional it is, it might be time to tear up that contract.

8.
the #1
mistake
parents make

One of the hardest things to do as a parent is to watch our children fail. And yet, failure is an inevitable part of all our lives. Failure is also an indisputable component of success.

The temptation is to correct the mistakes in their homework, finish their art and science projects so theirs can be the best in the class, and protect them from failure every chance we get. But all of these are parenting mistakes.

It's hard to watch them make mistakes, it's excruciating to let them fail, but little mistakes now massively increase the chances that they won't make big mistakes later, and little failures now massively increase the chances that they won't have big failures later.

The biggest mistake we can make as parents is trying

to prepare life for our children by smoothing the path in front of them. Our job as parents isn't to prepare the path for our children, it's to prepare our children for the path.

9.
does God
have a sense
of humor?

There are so many opportunities each day to catch a glimpse of the genius of God. One of my favorites is laughter. God is the genius behind humor and laughter. Laughter is essential to the human experience, and humor has been observed in every culture, in every place and time. Can you imagine life without laughter?

The goodness and genius of God is evident in laughter. Laughter is medicine for the body, mind, and soul. Its benefits are endless.

Modern medicine has discovered that laughter strengthens your immune system, improves mood, and diminishes pain. Laughter is a powerful form of stress relief. It burns calories, eases anxiety, reduces stress, and is a natural antidepressant. A good laugh relaxes the body, eases tension, and leaves your muscles relaxed for up to forty-five minutes. Laughter stimulates your heart and increases the number of endorphins released by your brain, which creates an overall sense of well-being. When you laugh, the amount of oxygen-rich air that rushes to your lungs increases. Laughter reduces blood pressure, increases blood flow, and can help protect you from a heart attack. It increases happiness, reduces anger and other negative emotions, and increases resilience in the face of obstacles and unpleasant events. Laughter increases our energy and enthusiasm for life. People who laugh regularly are more joyful and have healthier hearts. Humor improves personal satisfaction, strengthens relationships, helps defuse conflict, shifts our perspective, and attracts other people to us. Laughter connects us with others, makes our burdens seem lighter, and can reduce anger and conflict. It creates a sense of belonging and bonds people together. It enhances teamwork and improves productivity. Laughter and humor build trust, encourage collaboration, increase likability, draw people in to listen, improve memory and retention, make arguments more persuasive, and increase learning by reducing classroom anxiety. Laughter releases serotonin, which improves focus, decision making, problem solving, objectivity, openness to new ideas, and overall brain-power.

It took some really smart scientists to discover all this, but God is the genius who is alive and well in laughter.

All this may leave us wondering: Does God have a sense of humor?

Humor is essential to the human experience. Many of the most memorable and meaningful moments in life are humorous. But where is humor in our experience of God, religion, and spirituality?

If you read the life and teachings of Jesus as portrayed in the four Gospels, there is little evidence to suggest that he had a sense of humor. Do you believe that Jesus didn't have a sense of humor? I believe he had a wonderful sense of humor. I imagine him walking down the dusty roads of Galilee with his disciples. Thirteen guys spending all that time together. There must have been some epic moments of humor. Wouldn't you love to hear Jesus laugh? Wouldn't you love to know what made him laugh and how he made others laugh?

For some reason, nobody thought it was important enough to record, and we have been making the same mistake by excluding humor and laughter from our relationship with God ever since. Just as humor is essential to the human experience, maybe it is also essential to our spiritual experience.

There is an old joke about making God laugh. It is often repeated and rarely questioned, but we will question it together now. "If you want to hear God laugh," the joke goes, "tell him your plans." If you think about it, this theory is tragically flawed. What kind of father would laugh at his children when they tell him their plans? In the joke, God is laughing at us—or is he laughing at our plans, or our innocence, or our ignorance, or our arrogance? What kind of God would laugh at his children in any of these ways? Not the God I believe in.

I am a father, a broken and imperfect father, but I cannot imagine laughing at my children's plans. The Scriptures tell us that God delights in his children. And God has taught me to delight in listening to what is going on inside my children's hearts and minds. When they honor me by sharing their hopes and thoughts, I am fascinated. How much more does God, in his infinite goodness, delight when we open our hearts and minds to him?

So, it is impossible for me to conjure an image of a God who laughs at his children or their plans, however misguided they may be at times. But it is equally impossible for me to subscribe to an image of a God with no sense of humor. Does the God who gave us laughter not laugh himself? Does the God who gave us laughter have no sense of humor?

Absolutely not, and I yearn to know the God who gave us laughter.

10.
how to
find
yourself

The biggest mistake we make when we set out to find ourselves is to think that we need to do something. If we are looking to find ourselves it means we are confused and in search of clarity. Some people set off to travel the world in a quest to find themselves and most fail, because the adventure becomes a distraction to the work at hand: finding themselves.

I will share with you the secret to finding yourself. Do nothing. Find a quiet room, a comfy chair, and sit in silence. Do this every day for as long as you can spare, and I promise, you will see visions and dream dreams, and your best, truest, most gifted and capable self will emerge.

Clarity emerges from silence. What could be more important than finding yourself? Everyone who loves and cares for you wants that for you, and it is a sign of wisdom that you want it for yourself. Give yourself the gift of silence each day and your unique and wonderful self will emerge. It has no choice.

11.
is your
life
working?

Is your life working? It's a simple question, really. We cannot look at another person's life and know, but most of the time, we know how well our own life is (or isn't) working.

When we reflect upon our lives, we usually discover that in some ways they are functioning well and in other ways they are dysfunctional. What does this mean for you? It means in some ways you are flourishing, but in other ways, you are experiencing dissatisfaction. God is speaking to you through that dissatisfaction. You can learn to live with your discontent, or you can accept it as an invitation.

The danger zone is marked by comfort. This is where things aren't great, but they aren't horrible either, so you just continue to muddle along. We gravitate toward comfort, and it's amazing how comfortable we can get with things that are uncomfortable or worse. The thought of something new and unknown activates our resistance and hesitancy. These are mental, emotional, and spiritual obstacles that we all need to push through in order to move from surviving to thriving. Are you thriving or just surviving? It's time to stop muddling along.

If your life isn't working, what are you willing to do about it? Are you open to trying something new? This is an invitation to flourish and thrive like never before.

12.
one minute
that will
change your life

My five-year-old, Ralph, came into my study to say goodnight last night. I gave him a huge hug and kiss—he is just delicious—and I said to him, "I love you for two forevers!"

"No, Daddy!" He replied.

"What do you mean?" I asked.

"There is only one forever!"

"Really?" I asked.

"Yep. This life is not forever! We are just passing through this life. The only forever is in Heaven."

Okay. Let's take a seat and sit with that. This is a five-year-old saying, "This life is not forever! We are just passing through this life." Powerful!

Take one minute each day to remind yourself that you are just passing through this life and that soon you will be dead, and I guarantee you, you will live more intentionally with passion and purpose.

13.
how to
make sense
of everything!

If you want to understand anything, begin with purpose. If you want to understand yourself, begin with purpose. What are you here for? What's your purpose? You are here to become the-best-version-of-yourself. This is your essential purpose, and everything makes sense in relation to your purpose.

What makes a good friend? Someone who helps you become a-better-version-of-yourself. What is the essential quality of good food? It helps you become the-best-version-of-yourself. Good entertainment—books, movies, music—help you fulfill your purpose. What is the primary purpose of work? To make money? No, making money is the secondary outcome. The primary value is that when you do good work, you become a-better-version-of-yourself.

Everything makes sense in relation to your essential purpose. Next time you have a choice to make, simply ask yourself, which option will help me become the-best-version-of-myself? You will be astounded at the clarity this one question will bring to your heart and mind.

Embrace, nurture, celebrate, defend, and take joy in the-best-version-of-yourself!

14.
how to become a more interesting person

"I don't feel very interesting!" someone said to me the other day, and I was fascinated with the comment. And I started wondering, "How does someone become a more interesting person?" This in turn got me thinking about the most interesting people I know.

I'm not very good at small talk and social situations make me a little anxious. But I love a great conversation. The question that has served me best over the years is, "What are you reading at the moment?" Many of the best conversations I've ever had started with a discussion about a book someone was reading.

But more and more I find that people don't read books, so I have a second question now, "What's your favorite podcast?" And this question has also given birth to some amazing conversations.

The most interesting people I know are readers. Or they listen to podcasts. Or both. They are always learning. That's what differentiates them.

So, if you want to become a more interesting person, get interested. Ignite your curiosity. Read books and listen to podcasts. And if you want to have some great conversations, ask people, "What are you reading at the moment?" or "What's your favorite podcast?"

15.
there are
two types
of people

The great predictor of success is not talent or opportunity, but attitude towards learning. Developing the habit of continuous learning leads to success both personally and professionally.

Benjamin Barber wrote: "I divide the world into learners and non-learners. There are people who learn, who are open to what happens around them, who listen, who hear the lessons. When they do something stupid, they don't do it again. And when they do something that works a little bit, they do it even better the next time. The question to ask is not whether you are a success or a failure, but whether you are a learner or a non-learner."

Become a life-long learner. It is essential in our quest to live more meaningful lives. Read books, take courses, listen to podcasts, and watch videos that help you become the-best-version-of-yourself.

16.
the #1 thing
i want for my kids
at school

Sometimes modern education seems like a form of brutality. To educate children requires strength, but it also requires gentleness. Their little souls need to be handled with care. We are all different, we all develop at different speeds, and we all have different gifts. When we try to force all children into the same mold, it bruises their little spirits and often kills their love of learning.

When we go for parent-teacher conferences there is one thing I always share with our children's teachers, "Our number one priority is fostering their love of learning. As parents, we want to collaborate with you (the teachers) in that great mission."

To love learning is a thing of beauty, a great gift, and something to marvel at. If a child loses his or her love of learning, it is so difficult to help them get it back.

I really don't care if my child is first in the class or last in the class. I am more interested in helping them develop a love of learning. If they love learning, I believe they will learn every day for the rest of their lives, and they will live rich and full lives.

Love of learning is a quintessential life skill. If you have lost it, it's time to reclaim it.

17.
the most important life skill

There are lots of life skills that can enrich our lives. Communication, creativity, problem solving, critical thinking, collaboration, leadership, adaptability, and the list goes on and on. But there is one life skill that is more important than all the rest. One life skill that will have the most impact on every aspect of your life: decision making.

Improve your decision-making skills and you will improve your life, relationships, health, personal finances, career, and every other area of your life. Decide today to become a phenomenal decision maker. It will change your life forever.

How? Here are 5 ways to become a better decision maker:

1. Take your time. Don't rush a decision, especially if it is a big one.
2. Be honest with yourself. Try to look objectively at the pros and cons. We are experts at deceiving ourselves, especially when we really want something. But desire creates blind spots.
3. Consider your options through the lens of your values and priorities. Will you be turning your back on the-best-version-of-yourself?
4. What are you missing? In most situations we don't see most of our options.
5. Study decision making. Read books about it, ask people how they make decisions, and observe your own process.

Invest in yourself by improving your decision-making skills. Becoming a phenomenal decision maker is the ultimate life-skill.

18.
the ultimate
and original
life hack

A life hack is a simple yet ingenious way of accomplishing something. But life hacks typically only apply to one specific task. The 80/20 Principle was the original life hack and remains the ultimate life hack, because it applies to just about everything.

What is the 80/20 Principle? Also known as Pareto's Law, the 80/20 Principle asserts that 80% of outcomes are the result of 20% of causes. The idea has been popular in business for a long time. For example, in business 80% of profits may be produced by 20% of products, or 20% of customers might account for 80% of sales. But the 80/20 Principle can be found almost everywhere you turn. 20% of drivers cause 80% of accidents. 80% of crimes are committed by 20% of criminals. 20% of words account for 80% of word use. 80% of pollution originates from 20% of factories. 20% of patients use 80% of health care resources.

But what does all this mean to you and your everyday activity? It means that 20% of your activities produce 80% of the positive results in your life. Do you know which activities make up the 20%? Because knowing that will change your life.

It's all about focusing on the vital few rather than the trivial many. But the reality is most of us tend to focus on the trivial many and neglect the vital few. We give our best time, attention, and energy to the things that matter least, and procrastinate about the things that matter most. We spend our lives doing the urgent things, rather than the important things.

Let me explain it in even more practical terms. Eight out of ten things on your to-do list will add little value to your life. Or to look at it more positively two of the ten things on your to-do list will add more value than the other eight combined.

Two are worth more than the other eight, but the tragic truth is we keep ourselves always busy with the trivial many and neglect the vital few.

Would you like to accomplish more by doing less? If so, make the 80/20 Principle your new best friend.

Resist the temptation to do all the little things first, start each day with whatever matters most. Give that your best time, effort, attention, and energy.

Your future self will thank you.

19.
the six-second
kiss
theory

Do you want to improve your relationship? How much time are you willing to invest to improve it? If six seconds could transform your relationship, would you be willing?

What you need is the six-second kiss. Kiss your partner for six seconds. Six seconds is longer than you think and most kisses last less than one second. One second is long enough for a passing connection and that's what most couples have—a passing connection.

The six-second kiss reduces stress by reducing the stress hormone cortisol, increases enthusiasm for life by releasing the love hormone oxytocin, builds an intentional bond between you and your partner, it's an exercise in mindfulness, and creates a ritual connection. Couples that kiss for longer are healthier, happier, and appreciate each other more.

So, kiss your partner twice a day for six seconds. That's 84 seconds a week. Make the six-second kiss a habit in your relationship, and you will be amazed how it transforms your relationship.

20.
the missing piece of your puzzle

Trying to put together a jigsaw puzzle without an important piece is incredibly frustrating. That is the story of millions of people's lives. Day after day, they are frustrated, but they don't realize they are missing a piece. They drive themselves crazy trying to put the puzzle of their own lives together without that critical piece.

The essential piece most people are missing is a vibrant spirituality.

You're a human being, a delicate composition of body and soul, mysteriously linked by the will and the intellect. The important word here is soul. You have a soul. It is literally your life force. When it leaves your body, you die.

It's time to start paying more attention to your soul.

Think about these four aspects of the human person: body, soul, will, intellect. We are obsessed with three of them: body, will, and intellect. We pamper our bodies, vigorously defend our right to decide the path we walk, and celebrate our individual and collective intellectual accomplishments. Yet, we often ignore the most important, the soul. Have you been taking care of your soul? Rate yourself between one and ten. Most of us neglect the soul in favor of the body. The body is constantly barking orders at us: Feed me, wash me, clothe me, pleasure me, feed me again, and so on. The body makes a continuous stream of demands upon us. The soul, on the other hand, is quiet and faithful. When the soul is hungry, our stomach doesn't rumble and growl. But it is important to feed our soul each day.

Yes, each day. How many days has it been since you intentionally fed your soul? You are a spiritual being having a physical experience in this world. Feeding your soul is the missing piece of the puzzle. There is no better time than right now to nurture your inner life, discover your spiritual needs, and feed your soul.

It is time to stop ignoring our souls. The soul integrates and harmonizes every aspect of our humanity. It reorients us toward what matters most.

21.
the first mistake
most people
make each day

The alarm clock goes off. It's time to get out of bed. This is your first decision of the day. Will you get out of bed or hit the snooze button? You press the snooze button and roll over.

What just happened? No big deal, right? Wrong. You just lost the first battle of the day. Resistance just kicked your butt. Resistance has broken your will before you've even gotten out of bed. You will most likely be its slave for the rest of the day.

What is resistance? It's that sluggish feeling of not wanting to do something that you know is good for you, it's the inclination to do something that you unabashedly know is not good for you, and it's everything in between. It's the desire and tendency to delay something you should be doing right now.

Don't be a slave to resistance. Start by slaying it in that first moment of each day.

And remember, don't just be yourself, become the-best-version-of-yourself!

22.
comfort
is killing
us

It's natural to turn to comfort during times of exhaustion and suffering. Comfort has its role to play, but what is the purpose of comfort?

The purpose of comfort is healing, rejuvenation, and renewal, in order to prepare us to face new challenges and opportunities in life.

But there is also a dark side to comfort. It is seductive. When comfort becomes the goal of our lives, we begin a debilitating downward spiral. Once we are addicted to comfort, it shifts from strengthening us to weakening us.

Comfort is a beautiful servant, but an ugly master. It will destroy you if you let it. It will sap your soul strength, leaving you morally, ethically, and spiritually paralyzed... which will prevent you from standing up for what is good, right, true, and just.

Once you start living for comfort, there is no amount of comfort that will satisfy you.

23.
how is
comfort
killing you?

If you want to destroy people, make them comfortable. Give them every comfort they desire. Love of comfort poisons the soul by reducing our ability to hear truth and align our lives with it.

When we hear truth, we have one of two reactions. If we are living the truth we hear, we delight in the splendor of it. If we are not living that truth, we become uncomfortable, because unlived truth is always an invitation to change.

And let's face it, there is plenty of truth we aren't living.

A lover of comfort closes himself off from truth because it isn't comfortable. He will even avoid the truth that he knows will liberate him from his addiction to comfort.

Don't get too comfortable. Life isn't supposed to be comfortable. Constant comfort isn't good for us. Allow it to serve when you need to be restored and rejuvenated, but don't become a lover of comfort. Comfort will destroy you long before the difficulties of life.

24.
what
is
headtrash?

Do you feel like you aren't reaching your full potential? The problem could be HeadTrash. What is HeadTrash? HeadTrash is a collection of negative thoughts, self-defeating mind habits, and any other thoughts that take you away from the here and now.

HeadTrash leads you into self-limiting patterns of behavior such as: self-criticism, control, insecurity, judging self and others, procrastination, arrogance, paranoia, anger, fear, and unresolved guilt.

Sometimes we deposit this trash in our minds and sometimes other people deposit it in our heads. You may have HeadTrash that has been there most of your life, and HeadTrash that you collected today. Either way, it's time to take out the trash.

Anytime you feel stuck, trapped, or in a rut... the obstacle, at least in part, is probably HeadTrash.

25.
3 ways you sabotage yourself with headtrash

The important thing to remember is that HeadTrash is a form of self-sabotage. We do it to ourselves. Other people may contribute, but we have more control over our thoughts than anything else in our lives or in this world.

We make ourselves and design our lives with our thoughts. Thought determines action, action determines character, and your character is your destiny. It all begins with the seed of thought.

Self-sabotage is one of the greatest sources of unhappiness in our lives. We sabotage our relationships, personal finances, career, health, and so many aspects of our lives when we engage HeadTrash.

Here are three ways we all sabotage ourselves with Headtrash:

1. Self-limiting beliefs. We all have them. What are yours? What do you believe about yourself that isn't true?

2. The Voice of Negativity. This voice within you always has a reason why you can't do something, be more, become more, love more, receive more. There are two mistakes we make when it comes to the voice of negativity: we believe it and we dialog with it. Don't dialog with it. You cannot win that argument. You can never win an argument with someone who doesn't actually exist.

3. Need to Be Right. Sometimes we would rather be right than happy, we would rather be right than successful, we would rather be right than live life to the fullest. We will fail in order to prove a point. The desire to be right over other good things is pure HeadTrash. Dispose of it.

26.
are you having a midlife crisis?

What society calls a midlife crisis isn't a crisis at all. It's natural. It's normal. It's the passage from the first half of your life to the second half of your life. This is a good thing. Don't avoid it. Don't ignore it. That's the biggest mistake you can make. Don't put it off. Embrace it. You'll be glad you did. It's only a crisis if you pretend it isn't happening.

The first thing to realize about the midlife experience is this... If you are having what they call a midlife crisis you should be celebrating that, because for most of human history you would have been dead by now. The glass is not half full, and it is not half empty. Your cup overflows.

Are you having a midlife crisis or a midlife opportunity? You get to decide.

27.
13 signs you are having a midlife crisis

Do things seem a little off? You may be having a midlife experience. Is it a crisis? Maybe. Here are 13 signs you might be having a midlife crisis:

1. You feel trapped.
2. You don't know what you want.
3. Your life doesn't make sense anymore.
4. The things that used to satisfy you no longer satisfy you.
5. You're experiencing mild or severe depression, or unusual mood swings.
6. You have a growing sense that there must be more to life.
7. Shifting sleep patterns: You don't feel like getting out of bed in the morning or have trouble falling asleep at night.

8. You start questioning the big decisions you have made.

9. You begin to question your priorities, values, and what you want from life.

10. You have trouble making even the smallest decisions.

11. Everything and everyone frustrates you, including yourself.

12. Increased compulsivity around food, drugs, alcohol, sex, shopping, or anything you consider a relief from the constant and mounting anxiety.

13. You have a sudden urge to lose weight, get in shape, look better, and feel better.

Are you having a midlife crisis or a midlife opportunity? You get to decide.

28.
how do you know if someone is a narcissist?

The term Narcissist is definitely overused in society today. If someone doesn't like another person or they get their way, they are quick to say, "He is such a Narcissist!" or "She is such a Narcissist!" At the same time, it does seem that the self-referential nature of our culture lends itself to more and more Narcissistic behavior, and that the number of Narcissists is increasing in society.

We all have Narcissistic tendencies, but that's different from being a Narcissist. So how do you know if someone is a certifiable Narcissist—that is, someone with Narcissistic Personality Disorder (NPD)—or just immature, self-absorbed, or selfish?

Experts seem to agree that as many as one-third of the population are Narcissists, but it is quite rare for someone to be officially diagnosed with Narcissistic Personality Disorder. The Diagnostic Manual for Mental Disorders (5th Edition) states that in order for a person to be diagnosed with NPD, that person must exhibit five or more of these nine criteria, and at least one aspect of their life must be impaired by these behaviors. The nine criteria are:

1. Exaggerates own importance
2. Is preoccupied with fantasies of success, power, beauty, intelligence, or ideal romance
3. Believes he or she is special and can only be understood by other special people or institutions
4. Requires constant attention and admiration from others
5. Has unreasonable expectations of favorable treatment
6. Takes advantage of others to reach his or her own goals
7. Disregards the feelings of others, lacks empathy
8. Is often envious of others or believes other people are envious of him or her
9. Shows arrogant behaviors and attitudes

If you are being abused at the hands of a Narcissist,

recovering from the abuse of a Narcissist, or someone you love is in one of these situations a great place to start is by taking inventory of the nine criteria above.

I would encourage you to do it on two levels. First, just yes or no, answer from the gut, "Does he exaggerate his own importance?" Yes or no. Don't overthink it. "Is she preoccupied with fantasies of success, power, beauty, intelligence, or ideal romance?" Yes or no. Work your way through the list and see how many of the criteria your Narcissist displays. Remember, someone can be a Narcissist and not technically have NPD. So just because your Narcissist only displays three of the criteria doesn't mean he or she is not a Narcissist.

Next, go back through the list of nine criteria and identify specific examples of where you personally witnessed that behavior and write them down. Don't make excuses for the Narcissist in your life. It's amazing how many excuses we make for Narcissists. Earlier I used the word abuse. How did you respond when you heard that word? It's amazing how often people will say, "Well, it's not really abuse." That's why Narcissists get away with all they get away with for so long, because we downplay it, pretend it isn't serious, and make excuses for them. We say things like, "She had a really tough childhood." So? A lot of people have tough childhoods and don't grow up to take it out on others by abusing them verbally, emotionally, psychologically, or physically.

Narcissism is real. We all have at least one Narcissist in our lives, and it is past time that we started to understand what drives them and how they are impacting our emotional health and our lives in general.

29.
recovering from a relationship with a narcissist

If you're trying to recover from a relationship with a Narcissist, the most important thing for you to understand is that you never had a chance. It is a truth that is both tragically sad and amazingly liberating. Sad because you have and are suffering. Liberating because it proves that there is absolutely nothing you could have done to prevent this relationship from failing. It is not your fault. The first truth about being in a relationship with a Narcissist: You never had a chance.

I set this conversation in the past, because I hope you have ended your relationship with the Narcissist in your life. But the truth is you may work with him, you may have children with her, and even if you never have to see or speak to your Narcissist ever again, that person will always be in your life. I'm sorry, but that's just the cold, harsh, truth. So, let's put it out there and deal with it. There is no point pretending.

Narcissists have plagued my life. They have hurt me in ways I didn't even know were possible. It is dizzying how quickly a Narcissist can move from charm to harm, and back to charm again... and then pretend that the harm never took place... or that it was your fault.

Just don't be drawn into the state of mind that gets you thinking you could have done something to save that relationship. Remember the first truth about being in a relationship with a Narcissist: You never had a chance. Understanding this is the first step to recovering from a relationship with a Narcissist.

30.
12 things emotionally healthy people don't do

When people are emotionally healthy, they are happier, have more dynamic relationships, and tend to be physically healthier. Emotionally healthy people protect this happiness by doing certain things, but they also protect their health and happiness by NOT doing other things. Here are 12 things emotionally healthy people DON'T do:

1. They don't compare themselves to other people. They recognize this is one of the main sources of unhappiness and they avoid it.

2. They don't judge themselves (or their lives) by how they feel. You are not your feelings. Your feelings are not your life. Feelings play an important role in our lives but they are not the whole picture.

3. Emotionally healthy people don't expect other people to read their minds.

4. They don't react, they respond. Victor Frankl wrote, "Between stimulus and response, there is a space. In that space is our power to choose our response."

5. They don't ruminate on negatives. Negativity is toxic to our hearts, minds, bodies, and souls. Emotionally healthy people find ways to get their minds off the hamster wheel of negativity.

6. They don't suppress their feelings. They allow themselves to feel their feelings, and they learn to process and respond to them appropriately.

7. They don't feel like they need to fix every problem. They set boundaries by knowing which problems are theirs to solve and which are not.

8. They don't believe everything they think. Our minds produce thoughts that are beautifully true, brilliant, and creative. But they also produce bizarre and irrational thoughts, thousands of them. Emotionally healthy people know that not all our thoughts are true.

9. They don't need to find meaning in everything or know the meaning of everything that happens

right now. They realize the meaning of something that happens today may not be revealed for 20 years or longer.

10. Emotionally healthy people don't neglect their personal development. They never stop growing. They are committed to their personal development.

11. They don't try to control everyone and everything.

12. Emotionally healthy people don't allow guilt and failure to direct their lives. They cling to their hopes and dreams and allow love and goodness to direct their lives.

That's 12 things emotionally healthy people don't do. Which one do you need to work on today?

31.
15 things emotionally healthy people do

Without emotional health, happiness and overall satisfaction in life become almost impossible. And like so many of life's most important lessons, nobody teaches us these things. Here are 15 things emotionally healthy people do to stay emotionally healthy:

1. Self-Awareness. They observe themselves. They are constantly discovering new things about themselves and getting to know themselves more. Self-awareness is the first step toward emotional health, but it is not a once-and-done activity. It is the first step toward emotional health every day. When you practice self-awareness, you are able to see what habits and beliefs serve you and which do not. You can do so by

engaging in self-reflection and self-analysis on a regular basis. Observe yourself closely and deeply. Listen to your heart, mind, body, and soul.

2. Awareness of Others. Emotionally healthy people are aware of how what they do and say effects other people. They are able to put themselves in the other person's shoes, and as a result, they are quick to recognize the needs of others.

3. Emotionally healthy people question their assumptions about themselves, other people, relationships, and life in general.

4. They allow themselves to be angry. Most of us were told at some point in our lives that anger is bad or not to lose our tempers. But anger isn't bad. It just is. It's part of the human condition. You are angry about something right now. You may have been angry about it for 5 minutes or fifteen years. One thing is certain, the anger will stay, until we find healthy ways to process it.

5. They set boundaries by saying no. They are able to say no without feeling guilty, because they know what they are saying yes to. The only way to say no to anything is to have a deeper, more important yes. You may think you could never

say no and not feel guilty. That may be true in the beginning. But the first step is saying no, even if that means saying no and feeling guilty. Better to say no and feel guilty than to say yes to the wrong things. Emotionally healthy people also understand that other people use guilt to get what they want because it works, and they take themselves out of those manipulations by saying no.

6. Emotionally healthy people realize everyone is carry a heavy burden. They have large stores of empathy and give people the benefit of the doubt.

7. They know how to be alone. They enjoy their own company. They would rather be alone than hang out with people who are a negative impact on their lives.

8. Emotionally healthy people make decisions based on values not feelings.

9. They walk away from toxic people.

10. They are comfortable with uncertainty. They would rather wait for the right answer than rush to the wrong conclusion for the sake of having false closure.

11. They accept that everyone experiences stress, fear, anxiety, and depression at times in their lives. They don't see these as human malfunctions, but as highly tuned systems designed to help the human person avoid danger, get back on track, and thrive.

12. When they meet someone they don't like, they explore what it is about that person that makes them uncomfortable, and how that encounter might be challenging them to grow.

13. They have a healthy sense of self. They know who they are and who they are not, and they don't let other people determine their self-worth.

14. Emotionally healthy people understand that people come into their lives for reasons and seasons. Just because you were best friends once, doesn't mean you need to be best friends forever. Reasons and seasons.

15. They believe in the best of their humanity. They know in each moment they can choose to love, be generous, show compassion, and make a difference. They let the best of their humanity shine bright and often.

It is easy to neglect our emotional health, but the symptoms are unavoidable. They will emerge in every aspect of our lives and every relationship. Make your emotional health a priority by focusing on these 15 attributes, and you will develop a stronger sense of self and have healthier relationships.

32.
5 great lessons from roald dahl

My favorite movie as a child was *Willy Wonka and the Chocolate Factory*. Roald Dahl was one of the great storytellers of the 20th century. If he were alive today, he would be 105 years old.

Here are five quotes and five lessons he taught me:

1. From *Charlie and the Chocolate Factory*: "A little nonsense now and then, is cherished by the wisest men."

   Lesson: Life can get very serious at times. Lightheartedness and humor are essential ingredients for thriving and therefore cherished by the wise.

2. From *Danny, the Champion of the World*: "I will not pretend I wasn't petrified. I was. But mixed in with the awful fear was a glorious feeling of excitement. Most of the really exciting things we

do in our lives scare us to death. They wouldn't be exciting if they didn't."

Lesson: We are often most afraid when we are on the brink of great new achievements and experiences.

3. From *The Twits*: "You can have a wonky nose and a crooked mouth and a double chin and stick-out teeth, but if you have good thoughts it will shine out of your face like sunbeams and you will always look lovely."

Lesson: Few things have more impact on our lives than our thoughts. Spend as much time as possible thinking about beauty, goodness, and wisdom.

4. From *The Witches*: "Real witches dress in ordinary clothes and look very much like ordinary women. They live in ordinary houses and they work in ordinary jobs."

Lesson: There are some people in this world who will intentionally try to hurt you, but they can be hard to spot at first.

5. From *The Minpins*: "Those who don't believe in magic will never find it."

Lesson: Life is constantly unveiling new opportunities, new ideas, new experiences, and new possibilities. Stay open!

Five quotes. Ten sentences. A lifetime of lessons. He was an amazing storyteller.

33.
4 signs you are on the right path

One of the things that keeps us from finding our way in this world and becoming the best-version-of-ourselves is our desire for psychological comfort. When we have thoughts or feelings that make us psychologically uncomfortable, we rush back to our old thoughts and feelings. The problem is they drag us back into the past. It's often the uncomfortable thoughts and feelings that are trying to lead toward our bigger, better future.

Here are four examples:

1. You feel lost. Great. The people who are really lost have no idea how lost they are. The fact that you are aware of it is a great sign. Listen to that feeling. Explore what it is trying to tell you.

2. You are angrier than usual. Excellent. This means you are probably getting in touch with your dissatisfaction. Listen to your dissatisfaction. It will teach you how to improve your life.

3. Your friends are driving you crazy. Friends drive us crazy for two main reasons: They are dragging us down or they are challenging us to grow, and we are resisting. Which is it? You may just need some new friends for the next season of your life. Most people are the average of the five people they spend the most time with.

4. You feel like you need to grow up. Whether you are 14 or 64, this is a great sign. Growing older and growing up are two different things. Growing up is about becoming your own person, establishing boundaries, and taking responsibility for yourself and your life.

These are four signs you are on the right path. They may be uncomfortable, but they come bearing wisdom. Remember, feelings aren't good or bad, they are just messengers. Listen carefully to the messages they are delivering, and they will lead you to a more fulfilling life.

34.
7 ways to overcome overwhelmed

If you're feeling overwhelmed, you're not alone. It is one of the most common emotions in our society. Here are seven ways to get beyond overwhelmed!

1. Take a walk. Exercise clears our minds. It literally helps our minds rearrange thoughts and ideas, relieves stress, and releases happy hormones in our bodies.

2. Talk to someone. Just telling someone what we are experiencing can change everything. Even leaving a voicemail saying, "Hey, just wanted to chat, feeling so overwhelmed today!" can be liberating.

3. Do. Delete. Delegate. Divide your to-do list into these three categories. Divide and conquer. This will help you focus on what's essential.

4. Tidy your space. Organizing your work or living space has a way of reorganizing our thoughts and feelings too.

5. Ask for help. It's a sign of strength and genius, not a sign of weakness.

6. Cancel everything that is non-essential on your schedule for a day or two, or a week if that is what is required.

7. Do something. Start doing something, don't allow feeling overwhelmed to paralyze you. Inaction will only take you deeper into the overwhelmed state. Pick one thing on your to-do list and do it. It's amazing how taking purposeful action can shift the momentum of your day.

We all get overwhelmed from time to time. This isn't the last time it's going to happen to you, but it is time to develop a strategy to deal with it.

35.
10 things we forget when we feel overwhelmed

Overwhelmed feels like being buried alive. It feels like you are drowning. It's a state of panicked anxiety and when we are in that space we are not thinking clearly. Here are 10 things we forget when we feel overwhelmed...

1. Not everything we think is true. Our mind plays tricks on us. What's the truth here? You cannot do it all at once. That's true. You cannot handle it all at once. That's true. You can handle it one thing at a time. That's the most important truth in this situation.

2. This is temporary. This too shall pass. You've been here before and you got through it. You will get through this.

3. You got this. You can do this. You know how to get through this, you know what you need to do, you just aren't thinking clearly at this moment.

4. You don't need all the answers and a total plan to move forward.

5. Feelings are not always connected to reality. Overwhelmed is a feeling. But you are not your feelings, and your emotions are not your life.

6. We forget to breathe. In stressful situations we sometimes hold our breath without even realizing it when what we need is the exact opposite. Oxygen makes clear thinking possible. Breathe deeply. Fill your body with the oxygen your mind needs to navigate this situation.

7. Doing nothing will only sustain these feelings of being overwhelmed. If nothing changes, nothing changes. Change something right now. Overwhelmed is a feeling of helplessness. Take back your power immediately. Do something to move you out of this state.

8. Gratitude changes our state of mind every time. What are you grateful for?

9. Our problems are usually not as bad as we think they are and not as unique as we think they are.

Ask any therapist. Other people in history have been through some version of what you are going through and they found a way...

10. It's amazing how quickly things can turn around. The smallest step in the right direction can shift the momentum of your life.

We all get overwhelmed from time to time. This isn't the last time it's going to happen to you, but it is time to develop a strategy to deal with it.

36.
recovering
from
trauma

Imagine for a moment that you were injured in an accident, and you had to learn to walk and talk again. It would be excruciating. Each half step, each syllable, would require all your concentration and effort. And then, there is the mental anguish of not knowing if you will ever walk again or talk again.

Recovering from any trauma is like learning to walk again. You have to focus on the basics. It is slow and can be excruciatingly painful and difficult.

But the hardest trauma to recover from is the one we don't even acknowledge as a trauma. What trauma, large or small, do you need to recover from? It may have happened last week or 20 years ago. It's important to name it so that healing can begin.

Whatever trauma you have suffered... Be patient with yourself. Be gentle with yourself. And celebrate every advance no matter how small.

37.
the ISMS
are destroying
us?

Philosophy means lover of wisdom. Are you a lover of wisdom? Do you believe the more wisdom you have the happier and more fulfilling your life will be? Most people don't, and that's why the ISMS rise up in every place and time and destroy people's lives.

The four practical philosophies ruling our age are:

Individualism. What's in it for me?

Hedonism. If it feels good, do it.

Minimalism. What is the least I can do?

Materialism. Material possessions are more important than character and values.

Every day you make hundreds of decisions. Are you trying to make wise choices or are you wrapped up in the ISMS of our age? Do you have a process for making decisions or are you just doing the best you can in each situation?

Let me share with you a way that will help you start making better decisions right now, today. Whatever the decision, just ask yourself: What will help me and others become the-best-versions-of-ourselves?

38.
baseball's greatest lesson

The greatest lesson baseball teaches us is how to fail. It may sound insane at first, but just as failure is an indispensable part of what made Albert Einstein a genius and Thomas Edison a genius, failure is part of baseball's genius too.

One of life's greatest lessons is that failure is a part of any great achievement.

Baseball teaches us more about failure than any other sport. With a batting average of .350, you are the best in the world. That means the best in the world fail sixty-five percent of the time.

While he was the Commissioner of Baseball, Fay Vincent described it perfectly when he said,

"Baseball teaches us how to deal with failure. We learn at a very young age that failure is the norm in baseball, and precisely because we have failed, we hold in high regard those who fail less often—those who hit safely in one out of three chances and become star players. I also find it fascinating that baseball, alone in sport, considers errors to be a part of the game, part of its rigorous truth."

Powerful insights. Failure is part of success. Mistakes are part of life.

39.
the hardest lesson to teach your child

The hardest lesson to teach a child is how to fail. It's especially hard because we don't want to teach our children how to fail, because we don't want them to fail.

Here are the problems with that:

1. Failure is part of success, so teaching our children to be successful requires that we teach them: how to fail, how to learn from failure, and most of all, to get back up and try again.

2. By not teaching our children how to fail, we actually teach them that it isn't okay to fail. This is one of the most disastrous beliefs a child can carry, because when children believe it's not okay to fail, they often don't even participate... and as parents we want our children to participate fully in life.

3. Children who are not taught how to fail, mistakenly believe "If I fail, I am a failure." And it isn't a matter of if they will fail, but when they will fail. It's just part of life.

And just as a child can make the mistake of drawing their identity from their successes or failures, as parents we can make the same mistake.

We don't want our children to fail, because we think it reflects badly on us and fear judgment. But the first principle of parenting is: it's not about us, it's about them.

Here's the bottom line: Failure is part of success. Learning to fail and get back up is an essential life lesson. A child that fails is not a failure. And you are not your child's failures.

40.
the
generosity
habit

Everyone knows the world is in need of profound change. We just can't seem to agree on the best way to go about that. But do we really think politics, education, law, economics, or technology are going to deliver?

It depends largely on what we are trying to accomplish. All these aspects of society should serve human flourishing, but our unbridled quest for more, bigger, faster, and better, seems to have blinded us to how change either ennobles or debases people.

Are you flourishing?

Is your neighbor flourishing?

Is our nation flourishing?

Is the human family flourishing?

The next big leap for humanity will come from re-discovering what it means to be authentically human.

It is the very best of our humanity that the world desperately needs now—and generosity brings out the best in people.

The generosity habit is simple: Give something away every day. It doesn't need to be money or material things. In fact, the philosophy behind the generosity habit rests on this singular truth: You don't need money or material possessions to live a life of staggering generosity.

Generosity is creative. There are an infinite number of ways to be generous without money or things.

Express your appreciation. Call someone you haven't spoken to in a while. Make someone's day. Speak your love. Teach someone something. Support local businesses. Host a dinner party. Say thank you from the depths of your soul. Spread a positive message. Be a generous lover. Give blood. Listen, really listen to someone. There are so many ways to give generously.

Imagine if everyone adopted the generosity habit. What's more likely to change the world? Generosity.

Again, the generosity habit is simple: Give something away every day. Try it. It will change your life in ways you cannot even begin to imagine.

41.
who do you need to forgive?

Everybody needs to forgive somebody. Someone probably comes to mind for you, but sometimes the person we most need to forgive is ourselves.

There is no path forward without forgiveness. Refusing to forgive is like drinking poison and expecting the other person to die. But it is a poison we have all taken.

Forgiving someone is one of the hardest things to do in life. And the more you love someone, and the more that person hurts you, the harder it is to forgive. Some days you feel you are making great progress, and then there are days when you feel further away from being able to forgive than ever.

What I find humbling is that it is my need to forgive, not their need to be forgiven. The person I need to forgive could be long gone, and no longer a part of my life. He may not have even thought of me in years. The need is mine, and I find it is healthy to remember that.

But there is no future without forgiveness, so whoever you need to forgive, perhaps it's time to set yourself to the task... especially if the person you need to forgive is you.

42.
how many sundays left?

My brother Simon is thirteen years older than I am. When I was a child, he used to sell life insurance, and he later went on to become a financial adviser. I dedicated my book *The Dream Manager* to him, because in many ways he was the first person to play this role in my life in a more formal way. He has a lot of stories, analogies, and paradigms that he uses to illustrate his philosophy about life and business. This is one of my favorites: How many Sundays do you have left?

I am 48 years old. The actuaries at life insurance companies tell us that on average American male lives to 78. On average, an American female lives to 81. These life-expectancy statistics are always changing. For example, in the year 1900, the average life expectancy was just 31 years.

Anyway, Simon loves to talk about how many Sundays are left. At 48 years of age with a life expectancy of 78, I have 1,560 Sundays left. It sounds like a lot, but they go quickly.

As Simon loves to say, "Don't waste a single Sunday. If you don't waste Sundays, you will be less likely to waste Mondays, Tuesdays, Wednesdays . . ."

43.
the secret
to the
good life

What is the secret to the good life?

Since Aristotle first spoke of "the good life" almost 2,500 years ago, it seems everyone has been on a quest to experience it. I have heard many people speak about it and I have read many books on the subject. Some people think it's about success and accomplishment. Others think it's about money and things. Some think it's about love and family. Others think it's about food, wine, travel, adventure, education, meaningful work, independence, friendship, and pleasure.

There's nothing wrong with these things, unless these things are all you've got. Because even all of these things together will not deliver the good life.

There is only one ingredient essential to the good

life. So essential that without it, the good life is impossible. You would think that such an ingredient would be widely sought after. It isn't. You might think that such an ingredient is scarce. It isn't. You may think this ingredient is expensive. It isn't. You may think people would be clamoring to get their hands on it. They aren't.

When people talk about the good life, you get the impression that it is mysterious and only available to a select few people. This isn't true.

There is no secret to the good life. It isn't a mystery. No exceptional talent is required. It isn't only for the rich and famous. It is available to everyone, everywhere, at all times.

What is the essential ingredient of the good life? Goodness itself. The secret to the so-called good life has always been right before our very eyes. If you wish to live the good life, fill your life with goodness. Fill your life with love, kindness, gratitude, compassion, and generosity.

Do good. Be good. Love goodness. Celebrate goodness. Spread goodness wherever you go.

Take risks with your goodness. Test the limits of your goodness. Don't just love, astonish people with your love. Don't just dabble in generosity, live a life of staggering generosity.

How would your life change if your only goal was to do as much good as possible?

44.
the secret
to success
at anything

Success at almost anything rests upon this single principle: Master the basics. Do the basics, do them well, and do them every day, especially when you don't feel like doing them.

It doesn't matter if it is sport, personal finances, physical fitness, marriage, parenting, military operations, small business, big business, or your spirituality... The same principal applies. Practice the basics with heroic perseverance.

This is one of the reasons most people don't become phenomenally successful. They lack the persistence to do the same things over and over, to focus on the smallest improvements in the most mundane parts of whatever it is they are doing. Success at almost anything is usually the result of being the very best at four or five things, and they are usually the basics.

Mastering the basics is the secret to success... at anything!

45.
essentialism:
what is
essentialism?

Essentialism is about giving priority to what matters most and letting go of what matters least. It's about asking the question: What is essential for your health, happiness, and wholeness? And it's about choosing the people and things that are essential for your health, happiness, and wholeness over the many trivial and superficial time and energy vampires that suck all the passion and purpose from life.

Are you ready to give priority to what is essential? Are you ready to start saying no to all the stuff that in the long run won't mean anything to anyone? Does the idea appeal to you? Does just hearing about it stir your soul? Then maybe, just maybe, it's time you became an essentialist.

Maybe a little less in almost every area of your life is the secret to the rare fulfillment that we all yearn for but so few of us find.

46.
the difference between an essentialist and a non-essentialist

Are you an essentialist? Maybe you are, maybe you're not, and maybe you're not sure. So, let's take a look at the difference between an essentialist and a non-essentialist.

The non-essentialist rushes around trying to be all things to all people. The essentialist tries to be a great friend to a few people. The non-essentialist engages in the undisciplined pursuit of more. The essentialist engages in the disciplined pursuit of less. The non-essentialist is never satisfied. The essentialist has taken the time to explore what will deliver contentment.

The non-essentialist thinks, "I have to." The essentialist thinks, "I choose to."

The non-essentialist thinks, "It's all important." The essentialist thinks, "Only a few things really matter."

The non-essentialist is constantly reacting to what's urgent. The essentialist focuses on what's important.

The non-essentialist says yes without really thinking about it. The essentialist says no to everything except what is essential.

The non-essentialist takes on too much and does nothing well. The essentialist does less and delivers excellence.

The non-essentialist's life feels out of control. The essentialist's life feels measured and manageable.

The non-essentialist feels constantly overwhelmed and exhausted. The essentialist has learned to enjoy the journey.

47.
can you look yourself in the eye? seriously.

It's amazing how we avoid ourselves. Can You Look Yourself in the Eye? Seriously. Can you?

Try this: Stand in front of a mirror each morning for one minute, look yourself directly in the eye, and listen to what the man or woman in the mirror says to you. It will make you uncomfortable. But it works. Your eyes will tell you something every single day if you listen.

What type of things will your eyes say to you? Things like... You know what you need to do. It's time for something new. Take a walk today. If you don't ask, you'll never know. This has to stop. Today is going to be a great day, try to enjoy it. Start paying attention to your needs. Go and see your doctor. You won't feel good about yourself if you do that. You need some time off. A true friend would never treat you that way. Call your mom. Do something to make someone else's day today. Take a risk. Run. Swim. Dance. Sing. Hope. Love. Dream.

Listen to what the man or woman in the mirror is saying to you. It will change your life.

48.
never forget these six truths

Every life has highs and lows. I've had more than my fair share of mountaintop experiences, but like everyone else, I live in the valleys and on the plains.

There have been storms in my life, and I know there will be more. Here are six truths that put things in perspective:

1. You cannot live a meaningful life by filling your life with meaningless things and activities.

2. Everyone is going to hurt you. Find the ones that are worth the suffering and heartache, don't let anyone harden your heart, and remember, that even with your best efforts to avoid it, you are going to hurt people too.

3. Don't complain. It's not attractive or productive.

4. Give people the benefit of the doubt. Life is difficult and messy, and everyone is carrying a heavy burden.

5. Death comes to us all. When death approaches, the person you have become meets the person you could have been. This is a humbling encounter. Don't wait for it. Meet with the person you are capable of becoming for a few minutes each day, then use your thoughts, words, choices, and actions, to close the gap between who you are today and who you are capable of being. This is the path that leads to a deeply fulfilling life.

6. Ignore your critics. Everyone has them. They will tear down in an hour what they couldn't build in a lifetime. But life eventually puts all critics in their place. With time critics become remote and unimportant. The people who love you don't care about what your critics care about; they care about you as a human being. Your critics, they don't see you as a human being. They have dehumanized you. They see something in you that unsettles something in them. So, they have to decide: attack you or investigate their own dark mystery. Most people don't know you well

enough to compliment you or criticize you, and it is the unseen moments of our lives that define us.

Allow these six principles to guide your life and you will live an uncommon life of fulfillment and satisfaction.

49.
a christmas message!

The world is becoming more confusing. Our culture seems intent on throwing everything into a huge stirring pot and what comes out is an unrecognizable , bland, and virtueless blob. This great loss of identity effects almost everyone and everything. Christmas is no exception. This confusion makes us unclear about who God is, unclear about who we are and what we are here for, and unclear about what Christmas is and how best to celebrate it. Still, our souls are hungry for the simple, and thirsty for what is good and true. We often find this in simple traditions.

We all have traditions. Many parents have a tradition of reading their children a story before bed. It is a beautiful tradition that can have an enormous effect on the life of a child. Many people have the tradition of watching football on Sunday afternoon, some people make it a tradition to attend the Opening Day of baseball each year, while others hold the tradition of vacationing in the same place every summer.

Traditions are a beautiful thing. We can learn much about ourselves by examining our traditions for they reveal what we value.

Christmas is especially a time of traditions. Midnight Mass, presents, the Manger, a Christmas tree, lights everywhere, generosity toward those less fortunate, and the gathering of as much family together around a table as possible, to name just a few.

One of my Christmas traditions is to make a pilgrimage to the Playhouse in the Park in Cincinnati for the annual performance of *A Christmas Carol*. First published just a few days before Christmas in 1843, it was a massive success from the very beginning.

A pilgrimage is a sacred journey. I chose the word deliberately. There are many reasons to make a pilgrimage. We make pilgrimages to ask God for a favor or miracle, to beg forgiveness, to gain spiritual insight into a particular situation, to learn something new, to deepen our relationship with God, to visit a particularly holy place, or to escape the distractions of daily life to focus on life's bigger questions.

For some it is just entertainment, for me it is a pilgrimage, but nobody can escape the messages that are so well woven into the story that they sneak past all our biases, objections, and prejudices, to brilliantly challenge us to examine our lives.

Ever since Dickens wrote *A Christmas Carol,* the selfishness of modern man has been gathering momentum. So, to place the dangers of selfishness in full perspective by reminding us of the past, the present, and the eternal future is ever more relevant today than when this timeless classic was first written.

Every year, millions of people all over the world attend a performance of *A Christmas Carol.* They are men, women, and children of all faiths, and some of no faith. The fallen away, the barely practicing, the faithful, and so many who have never had Christianity presented to them in an authentic and compelling way. They will all leave better for the experience.

Life is messy. We are each intimately aware of our own mess and just how messy the world can be at times. But fortunately, Christmas is a celebration of that moment when God placed himself in the middle of our mess.

So, wherever you are in your journey, whatever is

happening in your life, this Christmas I pray that you will invite Jesus into your mess, and that by doing so, you will find new hope, deep healing, and a joy that cannot be extinguished!

May God bless you and all those you love this Christmas, and every Christmas to come!

50.
25 questions that will transform you and your life

Our lives are a response to the questions we ask. Toward the end of each year, I like to reflect on the year that has been and the year that is to come. I plan a little and dream a lot. Between Thanksgiving and New Year's Eve, I exchange questions with a group of friends. The questions are designed to encourage and challenge us to make the coming year amazing.

It's amazing how the right question can change the direction of your life, provide instant and startling insight, and allow you to see things you have never seen before.

Here are the twenty-five questions I put together to share with my friends this year. I hope they lead you to new dreams, rare discoveries, and the best year of your life... so far!

1. When was the last time you felt fully alive?

2. What do you believe about your past that is keeping you from your future?

3. If you could only accomplish one thing next year, what would you like it to be?

4. What needs to be on your NOT TO DO list next year?

5. What are you dissatisfied with at this time in your life?

6. What do you need most from your friends next year?

7. How do you want to feel differently one year from now than you do today?

8. Are you serious about making this the best year of your life?

9. Who do you want to help in powerful ways?

10. How do you feel about the year ahead right now? Is that how you want to feel about it all next year?

11. If you retired on December 31st, what would you spend your time doing next year? What piece of that can you do even though you aren't retiring?

12. What ten books do you want to read next year? Make a list. Check them off one at a time.

13. Who do you want to love more and better than ever before next year?

14. Have you given up on some part of your life? Which part? Why?

15. If you could vacation anywhere in the world next year, where would you go?

16. If you gave one thing away each day for a whole year, how would your life be different?

17. What do you do that requires only 10% of you, and what do you do that engages 90% of you... or more?

18. If you knew you only had one year to live, what would you make sure you did?

19. What is something you have to do, for if you do not, your soul will start to die?

20. What's the one thing you could do every day next year that would make you a-better-version-of-yourself?

21. When were you happiest this year?

22. What is it that you really want? Do you even know? If you don't, that's okay. But if that's the case, isn't it time you spent some time in the classroom of silence working it out?

23. What are you proudest of as you look back on this year?

24. What three dreams are most important to you next year?

25. What are you pretending not to know? And why are you afraid to acknowledge it?

The right questions can change your life forever. I hope these help make next year the best year of your life!

51.
the best
is yet
to come!

Is your life unfolding the way you thought it would? I was paging through my high school yearbook recently. There were 161 young men in my graduating class, and fewer than a handful are doing what they thought, hoped, or dreamed they would be doing. Most of them are glad. When they were seventeen or eighteen, they didn't know themselves well enough to decide what they were going to do for the rest of their lives.

Life doesn't turn out the way we expect. In some ways it exceeds our expectations, and in other ways it disappoints them. There may be hopes and dreams that were part of the life we expected that we need to grieve because they didn't materialize. But there are also hopes and dreams we had when we were younger that we are glad did not come to be. We see now that we were ill-suited for them, and they were ill-suited for us. At the same time, there are things about the unexpected life that surprise and delight.

Life doesn't unfold as we plan. We all live unexpected lives in one way or another. But sooner or later, we have to decide how we are going to make the most of the unexpected life. It is then that we come face-to-face with two enduring truths: We cannot live without the hope that things will change for the better, and we are not victims of our circumstances.

You are not what has happened to you. You are not what you have accomplished. You are not even who you are today or who you have become so far. You are also who and what you are still capable of becoming. You are your realized and unrealized potential. God sees you and all your potential, and he aches to see you embrace your best, truest, highest self. He yearns to help you and to accompany you in that quest.

Wherever you are, whatever you're feeling, however life has surprised and disappointed you, I want to remind you of one thing: The best is yet to come! There are times in life when this is easier or harder to believe, but the best is truly yet to come. Open yourself up to it, so you can see it and embrace it when it emerges.

about the author

MATTHEW KELLY is a bestselling author, speaker, thought leader, entrepreneur, consultant, spiritual leader, and innovator.

He has dedicated his life to helping people and organizations become the-best-version-of-themselves. Born in Sydney, Australia, he began speaking and writing in his late teens while he was attending business school. Since that time, 5 million people have attended his seminars and presentations in more than 50 countries.

Today, Kelly is an internationally acclaimed speaker, author, and business consultant. His books have been published in more than 30 languages, have appeared on the *New York Times*, *Wall Street Journal*, and *USA Today* bestseller lists, and have sold more than 50 million copies.

In his early-twenties he developed "the-best-version-of-yourself" concept and has been sharing it in every arena of life for more than twenty-five years. It is quoted by presidents and celebrities, athletes and their coaches, business leaders and innovators. Though perhaps it is never more powerfully quoted than when a mother or father asks a child, "Will that help you become the-best-version-of-yourself?"

Kelly's personal interests include golf, music, art, literature, investing, spirituality, and spending time with his wife, Meggie, and their children Walter, Isabel, Harry, Ralph, and Simon.

Visit **MatthewKelly.com** for his Blog
and so much more.

Subscribe to
Matthew's YouTube Channel!

www.youtube.com/matthewkellyauthor

Imagine how many

holy moments

you will trigger by introducing this idea to six people!